R. Mello 2000

© 2003 Mandragora

Mandragora s.r.l.
Piazza del Duomo 9, 50122 Firenze
www.mandragora.it

Author: Nancy Shroyer Howard
Artist: Richard Mello

Editing & Typesetting:
Monica Fintoni, Andrea Paoletti, Franco Casini

Printed in Italy

isbn 88–7461–000–9

This book is printed on TCF (totally chlorine free) paper.

Nancy Shroyer Howard & Richard Mello

Exploring Tuscany's Chianti Countryside

Four Excursions out from Radda and Gaiole in Chianti

Mandragora

*With gratitude to Bruna and Foscolo
who introduced us to a new life in the Chianti.*

For a number of years, Richard Mello and I have lived in the southern hills of the Chianti region. Visitors ask us to suggest pleasant half-day drives or all-day outings—and for directions with maps. Here they are—with Richard's paintings and prints.

In the first half of this book, we offer four itineraries. In the second half, we point out what we love and admire about the sites you will be exploring—villages, farms and castles, the grape and olive harvests. You may want to read this part first.

We wish you memories to cherish.

N.S.H.

Contents

Richard Mells 2000

Let's Go

Driving the Chianti Roads

This book is written for visitors who travel by car, bicycle, or sometimes on foot—not buses. Buses are too big for these hamlets and narrow roads.

The Chianti Classico map, from tourist offices, shows the entire Chianti very clearly. There are many helpful signs: *autostrada* signs in green, highway signs in blue, inns and restaurants in yellow, historic sites in brown. The sign 'Fermata' is for a bus stop. 'Divieto di Caccia' means don't go hunting!

On our four maps, we have drawn the roads we recommend. Arrows on our maps suggest the best approach or view. Blacktop roads are well maintained. Gravel roads can be dusty and bumpy, but are fine for standard cars. We have not included farm lanes that require 4-wheel drive.

Drivers on the winding Chianti roads are generally excellent. Nevertheless, it is wise to keep snugly to your own side of the road because others, coming around a bend, might not. It is also wise to drive slowly. Usually there are no shoulders, and around any bend there may be bikers or hikers in the road—or tourists who unbelievably simply stop, or half pull aside, rather than search for a decent pull-off. You are welcome to drive up a private road when a sign offers direct sales (*vendita diretta*) or wine tasting (*degustazione*).

Towns and villages are small, and the number of tourists is growing. To be thoughtful to the long-suffering residents, please look for the parking signs they have put up—a big white P on blue. These direct you to a spot that is usually just a short walk to the center.

We have indicated gas stations. To fill a tank, say "Pieno (*pee.eh.noh*), per favore." When closed, some stations (Radda's, Gaiole's) turn on self-service pumps. At a machine near a pump, insert a bill, exactly as it shows you, into the slot with the number that matches the pump you select. At the top of the machine, a message tells you if the bill is accepted. Squirt the hose into your tank. Cross your fingers. If it works, risk a bigger bill.

Finding Food, Funds, and Phones

We have listed, in our four explorations, some of the spots we particularly enjoy. Times and names change, so we have included phone numbers. Reservations for meals and wine tasting are often essential. Usually the person who answers the phone speaks English or will find someone who does.

In *Tabacchi* shops, you can buy tobacco, candies, cards, stamps, bus tickets, and phone cards. To use a public phone, tear off one corner of the card before inserting it. A mobile phone can be very handy.

Generally, stores open by 9:00 or 10:00 a.m., close at 1:00 or 1:30 p.m., re-open at 3:30 p.m. or so, and close at 7:00 or 7:30 p.m. Stores close on Sunday. On Monday, stores have varied hours. All food markets close Wednesday afternoons.

Banks are open weekdays, *feriali*, from 8:30 a.m. until 1:00 p.m., and sometimes again at 2:45 to 3:45 p.m. On holidays, *festivi*, some are open in the morning until noon. Many have ATMs outside.

Restaurants close through the late afternoon, then serve dinner at 7:30 p.m. at the earliest. Most restaurants take credit cards. Generally tips are included in the bill, *il conto*, but if the service has been pleasant, you might add a little.

Bars stay open all day and into the evening, and offer coffee, drinks, sandwiches (*panini, pah.nee.nee*), and pastries. In some bars, you first look to decide what you want, then pay at the cashier, then take your receipt to the food and drink counters. Most restaurants and bars have bathrooms.

Four Easy-going Outings

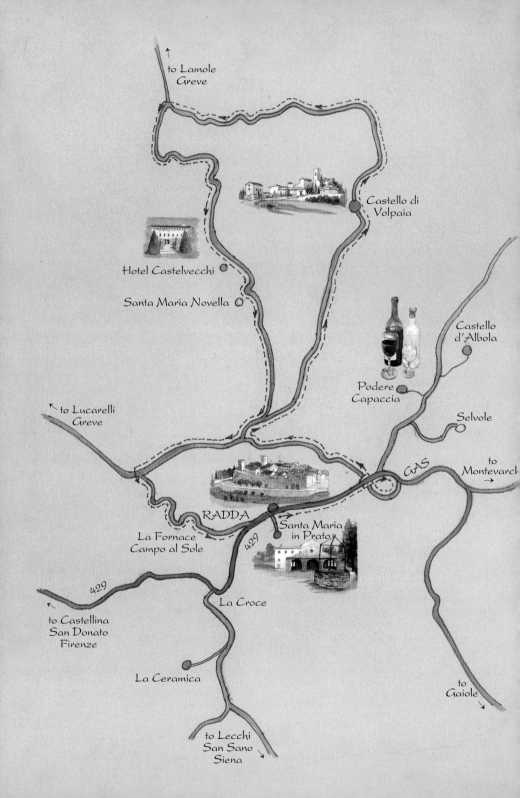

to Lamole
Greve

Castello di
Volpaia

Hotel Castelvecchi

Santa Maria Novella

Castello
d'Albola

to Lucarelli
Greve

Podere
Capaccia

Selvole

GAS

to
Montevarc

RADDA

La Fornace
Campo al Sole

Santa Maria
in Prato

429

La Croce

429

to Castellina
San Donato
Firenze

La Ceramica

to Gaiole

to Lecchi
San Sano
Siena

Chianti Exploration 1

Town of Radda in Chianti
Castle of Volpaia
La Fornace Campo al Sole, Kilns · La Ceramica, Pottery
Church of Santa Maria in Prato
Wine Tasting at Capaccia & Albola Vineyards

Town of Radda in Chianti
(rahd.dah een kee.ahn.tee)

The medieval town of Radda tops a high hill. It is possible to drive in a circle around the historic section, then stop at any blue parking sign. There is also parking, south side, below the Pizzeria Da Michele; stairs bring you up to the center.

Richard and I very much like to walk along the north wall of the town. Radda offers breathtaking bird's-eye views of the Chianti landscape. You will see working farms surrounded by their well-tended vineyards. You will also see farmhouses and barns that have been converted into vacation spots—with swimming pools—for visitors to this promised land. It is typical of the Chianti region that agriculture and tourism have achieved a symbiotic partnership.

Find the shady park and playground at the east end where you see the tall monument honoring "the sacrifice of our fathers." Looking across the street, you see the tower of this fortified town. Cross the street toward Porciatti and enter the street left of it. There are medieval tunnels on both sides that are fun to walk through, shops, and La Misericordia, the volunteer ambulance corps that has existed since the Middle Ages. Next, you enter the narrow central square.

In the 1200s, Radda in Chianti became one of the three centers from which large sections of Tuscany were administered. (The other two were Gaiole and Castellina.) Radda's prominent location provided a secure perch from which to oversee countless castles, their many outlying farms, vast agricultural resources, roads that carried the commerce of the region, and approaching enemy legions.

Nevertheless, Radda's town hall, Palazzo del Podestà, was destroyed in the Spanish Aragonese invasion of 1478 (see page 60). The town hall was reconstructed during the next three centuries. On the facade are the coats of arms of past potentates. Under the sturdy loggia, there is the tourist office with brochures on a window sill, a public phone, a sculpture by Leo Lioni, and a lovely fresco painted by a Florentine artist some 600 years ago.

The fresco depicts the Madonna and Christ Child with St John, who would one day baptize Jesus; John, who traveled in the wilderness, wears a shirt of fur. St Christopher is on the right. In legend, Christopher, a huge and strong man, carries a child across a turbulent river, steadying himself with a palm tree he has uprooted. Here, the child, holding the world in his hand, hangs onto the Saint's hair so he won't fall off. When Christopher learns he has just carried on his shoulders both the whole world and the Christ Child, he becomes a Christian—and eventually the patron saint of travelers.

Across the piazza is a fountain with a smiling lion, dribbling into a massive bowl and framed by a huge scallop shell. On the landing above, the church of San Niccolò provides the spiritual counterpart to the civic building below. Inside, lining both walls, are the fourteen Stations of the Cross (Christ's path to Calvary) on small blue and white majolica plaques. On these, you see Christ being forced to carry the heavy cross, others offering to help, the Crucifixion, and Christ carried to his tomb. Stations of the Cross are in many churches, but not always as nicely done. The Crucifix, created in the 1400s, presents a soulful, painfully thin Christ.

In Radda

Tourist office: in the town hall, Palazzo del Podestà, brochures and bookings. Open April–November, 10:00 a.m. to 1:00 p.m. & 3:00 to 7:00 p.m., Sunday 10:00 a.m. to 1:00 p.m. Staff speak English & German.
tel. & fax 0577 738494 e-mail: proradda@chiantinet.it

Coop food market, cafes, restaurants, *tabacchi*, wine-shops, banks, pharmacy, hairdresser/barber, dry cleaner (laundromat is in Siena).

Casa Porciatti Alimentari: delicious deli and meat market, great for a picnic, 8:00 to 1:00 and 5:00 to 7:30. Closed Wednesday and Sunday afternoon.
tel. 0577 738055 fax 0577 738234 website: www. casaporciatti.it

Trattoria Pizzeria Da Michele: fine pizza & Tuscan meals. Closed Monday.
tel. 0577 738491 fax 0577 738784

Le Vigne: country restaurant, on the right off road downhill, northeast out of Radda, lunch and dinner. Closed Tuesday, open all days Easter through October.
tel. 0577 738640 fax 0577 738809

Castle of Volpaia
(vohl.pah.ee.ah)

From central Radda, drive northeast, over a narrow bridge and, at the Y, veer right. At the stop, turn right, and pass under an arched bridge. In a mile or two, watch for the sign and right-hand turn to Volpaia. At a fork, veer right and follow signs to this hilltop castle. You will pass many of the outlying farms of Volpaia. The terrain and its scattered farms offer one of the hilliest and most beautiful landscapes of the region.

Just after taking a sharp left turn on the edge of the village, turn left into its parking lot. Walk down to a pretty cypress alley to see the small, walled cemetery, *cimitero*—then retrace your steps, walk toward the church, and up steps to the village square. There you see the tall castle's facade (with wine shop), a fountain, and a cafe.

Walking on old stone paving, circle the village and walk through at least two wonderful little tunnels. Though many of the castle's walls have long since been cannon-balled away, the atmosphere of a tough medieval castle can be sensed in Volpaia's tower, strong stone buildings, and the safe passageways over streets. In contrast, Volpaia's large, stuccoed villa, built in later years, has an airy garden within dense hedges.

Behind hefty wooden doors, Volpaia hides its modern wine-producing equipment. At its oil mill, *frantoio*, that processes olives of the region, perhaps you can see through glass doors in late fall the stainless steel machines that turn Chianti olives into delicious oil.

In Volpaia

Castello di Volpaia: daytime bar for coffee, sandwich or mid-day hot pasta. Open most every day. Wine, oil, group visits, and apartments.
tel. 0577 738066 fax 0577 738619 e-mail: info@volpaia.com

Casa Selvolini: apartments.
tel. 0577 738626 or tel. & fax 0577 738329
e-mail: casaselvolini@chiantinet.it

Before driving off, Richard and I like to look south from the parking lot to Radda on its hill, with its crenelated belltower—a splendid sight.

Leaving Volpaia, you have two choices. One is to drive right up through Volpaia village and onto the winding gravel road that loops north through dense chestnut forests, stopping at Castelvecchi Hotel (above) for a marvelous view (pulling off on the left). Or retrace your drive downhill. At the Y at the bottom, turn sharply right and drive on blacktop up to Castelvecchi for the view, passing the lovely church of Santa Maria Novella.

La Fornace Campo al Sole, Kilns
(lah for.nah.cheh kahm.poh ahl soh.leh)

Afterward, back at the main road, turn right and soon turn left at the first road. (There is a small sign beforehand: *La Fornace, Campo al Sole*.) At the Fornace, top of the hill, pull off on the right where you see piles of stones that once paved streets and squares. In the yard, you see traditional, hand-made terracotta products, including the huge jars that once stored oil. The old bricks and tiles are used in remodeled houses to help them fit into the landscape.

La Fornace Campo al Sole: tours available, drop-in but best by appointment.
tel. 0577 738040 fax 0577 738030 e-mail: campoalsole@chiantinet.it

La Ceramica, Pottery
(lah cheh.rah.mee.kah)

Take a sharp turn right onto 429. Shortly turn left—at a modern tile yard—toward Lecchi and San Sano. Watch for a sign, *La Ceramica*, on the right and go up a long gravel drive, following *La Ceramica* signs almost to the end. Here, Angela Pianigiani paints and sells her pottery. She works at a turntable, dipping brushes into bowls of colored glazes and painting whimsical flowers onto bowls, platters, pitchers, and vases.

La Ceramica: Angela Pianigiani, weekdays 9:30–12:00, 3:00–7:00, or weekends by appointment.
tel. 0577 738466 fax 0577 738072

Church of Santa Maria in Prato
(*sahn*.tah mah.*ree*.ah een *prah*.toh)

Return again onto the main road, 429, and drive into Radda. Turn sharp right, and go down and past Pizzeria Da Michele's parking, almost to the end. There you can relax at this lovely church.

The loggia along the front and side of the church provides a protected spot from which to catch glimpses of the landscape to the south, framed by cypress trees. The church itself is 11th-century. Inside is a panel painting of the *Madonna and Saints* by Neri di Bicci, a prominent Florentine artist of the late 1400s. In the 1600s, this became a Franciscan monastery. The complex has been recently renovated. Art treasures will be preserved in a museum at the back, now under construction.

Wine Tasting at Capaccia & Albola Vineyards
(cah.p<u>ah</u>.tchah & <u>ahl</u>.boh.lah)

A fine end-of-day event is a drop-in wine tasting at Capaccia or Albola vineyards. Drive northeast out of Radda. Immediately after the bridge, take the left fork toward Lucolena. Follow our map to each site.

Podere Capaccia: medium-size vineyard run by Giampaolo Pacini, drop-in wine tasting, all day.
tel. & fax 0577 738385
website: www.poderecapaccia.com

Castello d'Albola: large vineyard, drop-in wine tasting, 10:00 a.m.–6:00 p.m. Tour & brunch for groups of more than six, by reservation.
tel. 0577 738019

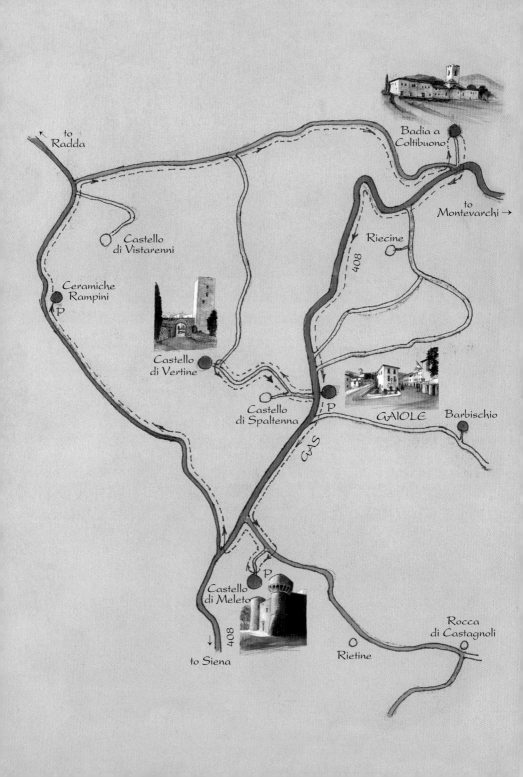

to
Radda

Badia a
Coltibuono

to
Montevarchi →

Castello
di Vistarenni

Riecine

408

Ceramiche
Rampini

P

Castello
di Vertine

Castello
di Spaltenna

P

GAIOLE

Barbischio

GAS

Castello
di Meleto

P

408

to Siena

Rietine

Rocca
di Castagnoli

Chianti Exploration 2

Town of Gaiole in Chianti
Castle of Vertine
Castle of Meleto
Rampini Ceramics
Badia a Coltibuono, Abbey

Town of Gaiole in Chianti
(gah.ee.oh.leh)

Visit Gaiole for a sense of an old market town. At the end of the so-called Dark Ages—the long centuries following the conquest of the Roman Empire in the 400s by waves of invaders—there began a rise of towns, travel and trade, beginning roughly in the 1000s.

Gaiole took shape in the valley of the Massellone river. Its lowland position and river made it an accessible commercial center. Into Gaiole came workers of the surrounding castles and farms, as well as merchants from afar. The river now runs in a canal, under the balconies of houses—very colorful when laundry is hung out—and alongside the main through-road, Via Roma.

In the 1200s, Florence divided the region into thirds and Gaiole administered one third. Today, Gaiole administers a large rural region, now a province of Siena. To the town hall, *Comune*, everyone in the township of Gaiole comes for permissions to turn farm buildings into dwellings, alter exteriors or interiors, or change the color of a building's stucco.

During recent years, Gaiole transformed its main square, on Via Ricasoli. Cars were moved out, old paving hauled away, new utility lines dug, and new paving laid down. Around the square, you can find shops and sustenance. Buildings are being given new stucco.

From Gaiole, a side trip to Barbischio is marvelous because as you ascend the hairpin road you see the hamlet—a castle actually—hanging onto the side of the hill—a thrilling Tuscan site. The houses are quite original and the tower was artfully restored.

In Gaiole

Gaiole's tourist office is in a building with round windows, on the left as you enter Gaiole from the south.
tel. 0577 749411

Around and near Gaiole's square: fine food & clothes shops, banks, shoemaker, *tabacchi*, hardware store, cafes, butcher, hairdresser/barber and wine shops. A pizzeria is above the square.

Lo Sfizio di Bianchi: family-run restaurant, bakery, and catering on Gaiole's main square. Homemade ice cream! Closed Tuesday.
tel. 0577 749501

Carloni: family restaurant, beyond the square, left off of Via Roma at 24 Via Giacomo Puccini. Closed Wednesday.
tel. 0577 749549

Castle of Vertine
(vehr.tee.neh)

On the main road in Gaiole, Via Roma, turn left beside the church with the handsome Gothic-style belltower. Climb to the sign and turn right for Vertine.

(Going straight, you can visit Castello di Spaltenna—once a fortified monastery with a parish church and now a four-star hotel and restaurant.)

Park on the road outside Vertine. You will see there a wonderful way to honor the hamlet's war heroes: three rows of deep-green holm oaks, play equipment for children, and a picnic table where families can relax. We believe the heroes listed on the monument would be pleased to see these: the soldiers, the sick and unlucky, the civilians, and—most haunting of all—the simply missing, *dispersi*.

Walk through Vertine Castle's arched entrance. Fortified by walls and tower, Vertine survived centuries of wars to stand as an example of medieval military architecture. It now is a picturesque spot with flowers, restored tower, stone-paved street, a terrace with views toward Radda, and no shops. We admire—and sometimes sketch—its brick-decorated church and weathered lions. You can return to Gaiole the way you came.

Castle of Meleto
(meh.leh.toh)

Drive south out of Gaiole and turn left at the sign for Castello di Meleto. Pass Meleto's modern *cantine* and the Maniera shop on the right, then turn right at the Meleto sign. Drive up the hill to the castle.

Meleto, once a Ricasoli Firidolfi castle, became a Florentine military post that was attacked and even occupied by Sienese troops in three centuries of conflict between the two city-states, beginning in the 1200s. As with so many castles here, Meleto was partially demolished by the Spanish in 1478, rebuilt by Florence, and again seriously damaged in the mid 1500s by troops of Charles V, Holy Roman Emperor.

After 1555, when Siena surrendered to Florence, relative peace reigned. Meleto was eventually transformed into a comfortable villa. Two massive, round 15th-century towers still stand. Inside the castle, several walls were elaborately frescoed, and in 1742 a little theater was created. Tours are available.

Leaving Meleto, you may want to see the work of fine Tuscan artisans in the shop, Maniera, below Meleto.

At Meleto

Castello di Meleto: gift and book shop, tours from Easter to end of October, in English & Italian, weekdays: 11:30 a.m., 3:00 & 4:30 p.m. (German except Thursday), & some weekends. Small fee. Apartments, Tuesday cooking class. Wines may be tasted.
tel. 0577 749129 fax 0577 749762
website: www.castellomeleto.it e-mail: info@castellomeleto.it

Below Meleto

Maniera: shop & showcase of Tuscan artisans in what was once an abandoned brick kiln.
tel. 0577 744023

Rampini Ceramics
(rahm.pee.nee)

Returning to the main road, turn left. Shortly after, at a fork in the road, make a sharp right turn. After a few curves up a hill, the ceramics studio and shop of the Rampini family appear on the right.

The showroom and shop are in the old ochre-stuccoed farmhouse. There, you will notice pottery in traditional Renaissance designs, but also unique Rampini designs that you will see nowhere else, beautifully painted in rich colors.

Ceramiche Rampini: hand-painted ceramics shop. Open all day, weekdays; in May through October open Saturday & Sunday. Custom orders. Complete place settings, bowls, platters. Shipping perfected.
tel. 0577 738043 fax 0577 738776 e-mail: info@rampiniceramics.com

Before leaving, Richard and I like to gaze at the amazingly patterned hillside behind Ceramiche Rampini. The 16th-century Castle of Vistarenni is at the top of the hill.

With great care, turn right out of Ceramiche Rampini. You might want to stop at Vistarenni Castle for a pleasant country walk. If so, turn in to the castle's driveway and park immediately on the right. Vistarenni Castle and its wine shop lie one mile up, at the end of this shady, cypress-lined lane. You can also drive up.

Back on the main road, just after the driveway to Vistarenni, turn right toward Montevarchi. Along this road, you will see newly planted vineyards and restored farmhouses.

At the sign for Badia a Coltibuono, turn left.

Badia a Coltibuono
(bah.dee.ah ah kohl.tee.boo.oh.noh)

On the driveway to the abbey, *badia*, you will see its shop, L'Osteria, on the right, where its wines and oils are sold. The abbey is straight ahead.

The Badia commands a hilltop of 500 meters. The first traces of the abbey date from 770, a Firidolfi holding, long gone. It is the 12th-century bell-tower and rounded apse of the Romanesque church that greet you as you arrive. The prosperous Vallombrosian abbey, benefiting from bequests and extensive farms and woodlands, came under Florentine protection in the 1200s.

During successive centuries, a cloister was added, frescoes were painted in the refectory, and a vaulted ceiling was put into the church. In 1710 two new wings and a lovely formal, geometric garden were added. Napoleon's conquest of the region and his edict closing the abbey in 1810 caused it to become a parish church and farm. Since 1842, the Badia a Coltibuono has been owned by the family of the present owner, Piero Stucchi Prinetti. His wife, Lorenza de' Medici, author of lavish books on Tuscan cuisine, runs a famous cooking school here. Tours are available. There is a fine restaurant, and on its left is a path for a woodland walk.

Nearby, at Cetamura, an archeological dig has been unearthing the remains of an Etruscan village, dating centuries before Christ.

Return on the main road to Gaiole, or through Vertine, or on smaller roads passing the Riecine vineyards—all picturesque drives.

Badia a Coltibuono: tours, May through October, Monday to Friday 2:30–4:00, except all of August & holidays. Small fee. Group tours & tastings by arrangement.
tel. 0577 74481 fax 0577 749235
website: www.coltibuono.com e-mail: pr@coltibuono.com

Restaurant: closed Monday, lunch and dinner May through October.
tel. & fax 0577 749031 e-mail: ristbadia@coltibuono.com

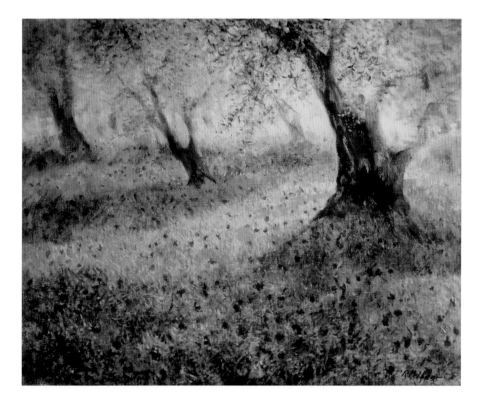

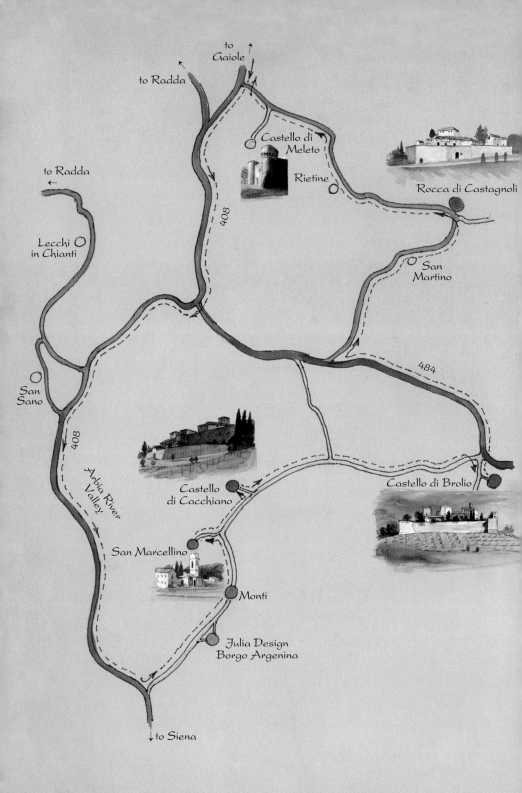

to Gaiole

to Radda

Castello di Meleto

Rietine

Rocca di Castagnoli

to Radda

San Martino

Lecchi in Chianti

408

San Sano

484

408

Arbia River Valley

Castello di Cacchiano

Castello di Brolio

San Marcellino

Monti

Julia Design Borgo Argenina

to Siena

Chianti Exploration 3

Village of Monti in Chianti
Castle of Cacchiano
Castle of Brolio
Fort of Castagnoli

Village of Monti in Chianti
(*mohn.tee een kee.ahn.tee*)

Pick up route 408, south from Radda or Gaiole, or north from Siena. Route 408 travels down the valley through which Florentine and Sienese troops trudged as they fought over the Chianti region (see pages 51–53). You can see that the flat valley floor lends itself today to fields of grain, legumes, and sunflowers. Turn at the sign for Monti in Chianti.

If you want a picturesque up-hill excursion on gravel, turn right at the sign for the inn, Borgo Argenina, and Julia Design. After visits, continue on this road down to Monti.

Pass the turnoff to Monti di Sotto and drive into Monti in Chianti. Look for the parking lot on the left; park and walk around. Here you can see typical modern building practices: stucco over cement block, accents in stone and brick, and balconies front or rear for plants and laundry. A shop for fine linens and embroideries, *ricami*, has a special kind of Tuscan garden in front: potted trees and flowers placed on gravel—cool and inviting.

Walk up the hill toward the church steeple, alongside the new sports-field's stone wall. On these walls, I like to explore the textures and colors in Tuscan stone that give houses and walls their cherished patina.

The parish church, or Pieve di San Marcellino, has two plaques on its facade, commemorating the dead of the two World Wars. A graceful olive branch, symbol of peace, is etched on one. The interior of the church is surprisingly decorative given the austere exterior.

Right of the church is a stone farmhouse that typifies an old Chianti *casa colonica* in its nearly original appearance. At the top is the tower-like pigeon keep, *colombaia*. Roofs are tiled. The house, a cube, has small, shuttered windows that let in a modicum of light, yet keep out summer heat and winter winds. On ground level, where oxen would sleep, are arched entrances leading into cover for oxcarts. Behind, as you can see from the road, is a tiny stone pig and sheep sty, with little stone corrals—where fig trees now grow!

Across the road, entering an alley of huge cypress trees, you find the cemetery with its photos and flowers and a chapel where three heroes are honored—and where the handy water bottles and brooms are stored.

Up the road, just beyond the farmhouse, is a red-brick tabernacle in which stands St Anthony of Padua, holding his symbols: the Christ Child in one hand and lilies, sign of purity, in the other.

Approaching Monti, Argenina Hamlet

Borgo Argenina: spectacularly-sited inn.
tel. 0577 747117 fax 0577 747228 website: www. borgoargenina.it

Next door, *Julia Design*: hand-painted textiles
and furniture, interior design and renovation.
tel. & fax 0577 747280
e-mail: juliadesign@iol.it

In Monti

Ricami Artigianali: lovely embroideries
to order as curtains and linens.
tel. 0577 747006

Tabacchi & Bottega: little market.

In your car in Monti, return up this road. Just past St Anthony, you can turn left onto the gravel road to Colle, and visit, at the end of the road, the state-of-the-art *cantina* where Marco Ricasoli produces his Rocca di Montegrossi wine, named for one of the family's ancient castles. Next to it is the medieval San Marcellino church.

Rocca di Montegrossi Vineyards: wines and new oil sold directly.
Wine tasting by appointment.
tel. 0577 747977 fax 0577 747836
e-mail: Rocca_di_Montegrossi@chianticlassico.com

Castle of Cacchiano
(kahk.kee.<u>ah</u>.no)

Return to the main road and continue uphill to Cacchiano. This magnificent castle commands a hill of 500 meters. Not surprisingly, a few Roman remains have been found on Cacchiano's stupendous site. To buy wine, a *vendita diretta* sign will direct you to the right spot.

Cacchiano came into the Ricasoli Firidolfi family in the 1100s and became part of Florentine territory in 1203. Its location did not save it from bombardment by the Spanish in 1478, nor burning by troops of the Holy Roman Emperor, Charles V — with Siena's help — in 1529. Rebuilt above its old walls, around an open courtyard and well, it has a large Renaissance wing. Today, Baroness Elisabetta Ricasoli Firidolfi and her sons, Giovanni and Marco, oversee extensive vineyards. The label of Giovanni Ricasoli (*ree.kah.soh.lee*) is *Castello di Cacchiano*.

Castello di Cacchiano: wines sold directly. Group visits by appointment.
tel. 0577 747018 fax 0577 747157 e-mail: cacchiano@chianticlassico.com
Apartments via agency, Stagioni del Chianti, in Florence.
tel. 055 2657842 fax 055 2645184 e-mail: info@stagionidelchianti.com

As you continue on the road from Cacchiano to Brolio Castle, you will see dozens of farmhouses of the Ricasoli Firidolfi domain. They date back to the days of share-cropping when peasants worked the lands of the owners. Today, some dwellings house workers and managers of the two castles' enterprises, and other farms are rented out or have been sold.

Castle of Brolio
(*broh.lee.oh*)

Brolio Castle is increasingly spectacular as you approach it. Pass the gate to Brolio's *cantina*, unless you have an appointment there. Drive through a cypress-bordered lane up to the gate of the castle. Ring the bell for a visit around the outside. The sweeping views from the high walls are thrilling.

Brolio looks as castles are supposed to look — tall, towered, and crenelated at the top — unlike so many cannon-balled, fortified Chianti castles. This is because Brolio Castle, inside its ancient walls, is 'new.'

Brolio, like Cacchiano, became a Florentine fort in 1203. Allied with the Guelphs (pro-Papacy) of Florence, both Brolio and Cacchiano were occupied by the Ghibellines (pro-Emperor) of Siena in 1252. Brolio was occupied by Sienese troops in 1434, and finally demolished in 1478 by Spanish Aragonese, Sienese, and Papal troops. Rebuilt, the castle was attacked and occupied by forces of Siena and Emperor Charles V, during his siege of Florence in 1529. In 1555, Florence defeated Siena, with the turnabout help of the Emperor. It is a wonder that anything survived, yet there is the chapel of the 1300s and an ancient tower or *donjon*.

Florentine Grand Dukes of Tuscany began to rule Chianti, including Siena. The Ricasoli were restored to Brolio.

In 1860, Baron Bettino Ricasoli rebuilt Brolio Castle in the red brick, neo-gothic style of Siena. Although occupied by the German military in World War II, Brolio was not harmed. However, a member of the family describes watching from the ramparts as bombardments exploded among the villages you are visiting.

Today, the owner is Baron Bettino Ricasoli Firidolfi and Brolio is a major wine-producing firm. Below the castle are its huge *cantina* and a fine restaurant.

Castello di Brolio: castle visits, Monday to Friday, 9:00–12:00 and 3:00–6:00. Small fee. Group visits by appointment.
Apartments via same agency as Cacchiano Castle.
tel. 0577 7301 fax 0577 730225

Osteria del Castello: restaurant just below Brolio Castle, lunch and dinner. Closed Thursday. Run by a fine chef, Seamus de Pentheny O'Kelly.
tel. 0577 747194 fax 0577 747277
website: www.seamus.it e-mail: osteria@chiantinet.it

Fort of Castagnoli
(kahs.tah.nyoh.lee)

Drive down from Brolio, following signs to Gaiole until you come to a right turn at a sign to Castagnoli. Park for a pleasant walk around this fort, *rocca*, and the medieval houses clustered beside it.

As a Ricasoli fortification, Rocca di Castagnoli weathered the same attacks from the 1200s onward as Brolio, Cacchiano, and others—but withstood an attack by the Aragonese in 1479. It is reported that 400 soldiers threw their ladders up against the fort's walls, failed to breach them, and retreated. Castagnoli also survived Charles V in 1529. The road continuing from Castagnoli takes you past the little village of Rietine and Meleto Castle.

In Castagnoli

Pizzeria L'Alto Chianti: next to the church, lunch and dinner, pizza added at night. Closed Monday.
tel. 0577 731008

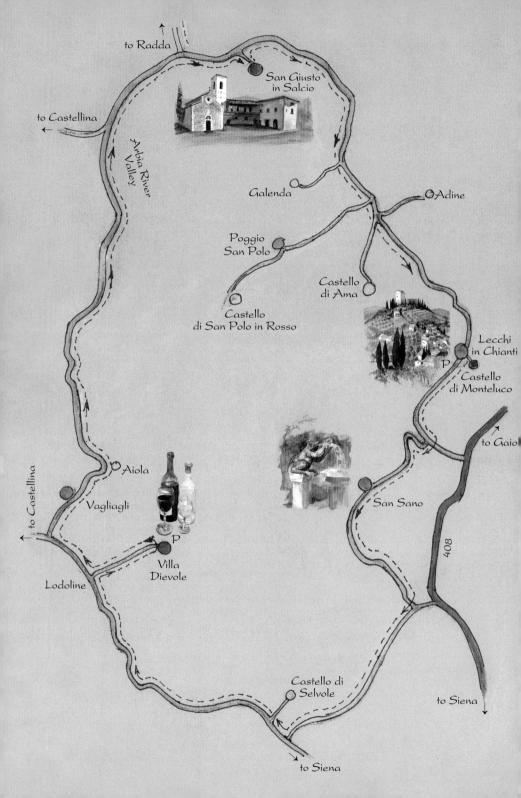

to Radda

San Giusto
in Salcio

to Castellina

Arbia River Valley

Galenda

Adine

Poggio
San Polo

Castello
di Ama

Castello
di San Polo in Rosso

Lecchi
in Chianti

P

Castello
di Monteluco

to Gaio

Aiola

to Castellina

Vagliagli

San Sano

P

Villa
Dievole

408

Lodoline

to Siena

Castello di
Selvole

to Siena

Chianti Exploration 4

Village of Lecchi in Chianti
Castle of Monteluco a Lecchi
Village of San Sano
Village of Vagliagli
San Giusto in Salcio Parish Church

Village of Lecchi in Chianti
(*lehk*.kee)

As you enter Lecchi's narrow street, look for the parking sign, 'Parcheggio', that puts you a few steps below the village, next to its metalworking shop (left) and woodworking shop (right). Please do not park on the narrow main street.

Lecchi is one of the Chianti region's many medieval hill-towns. It lies along a fairly high ridge. Lecchi's main street ascends up a cone-shaped hill to its protective tower and castle, Castello di Monteluco.

46

For centuries Lecchi was an agricultural village, with peasants, *contadini*, working their own small fields as well as the vineyards and olive groves of the region's castles and large farms. Older people in the village describe their lives before and during World War II as very poor—without running water, heat, electricity, adequate food—and walking miles to work or perhaps biking. At the same time, villagers reminisce about summer evenings together under the castle's shade trees—and the dances in its courtyard.

During World War II, Lecchi was occupied by German soldiers. Several families had to move out of their houses to camp in fields. One fellow was born in a ditch during a bombardment. Some seventy men and boys were marched away to work in German factories. Not all returned.

After the War, poverty was more severe in the region than before, continuing through the 1950s and '60s. Lecchi's population dropped from over 300 to 100 residents as Chianti's system of share-crop farming, *mezzadria*, collapsed and *contadini* headed to the cities, looking for work (see page 61).

It was not until the 1970s that Italy's economic recovery began to reach these rural villages. As Italians and other Europeans began to buy the abandoned farms and renovate them, village woodworking and metalworking shops were able to build new facilities and prosper. When tourism in Tuscany took off in the 1980s and '90s, Chianti's food markets, wine shops, inns and restaurants expanded or popped up overnight.

As villagers began to afford motorbikes and then automobiles, both husbands and wives could travel anywhere to work—to the big wine producers, to Gaiole or Radda, to Siena—yet could live in a rural village. In Lecchi, the population remains steady at just over 100 residents of all ages.

Particularly through the 1980s and '90s, families in Chianti villages such as Lecchi renovated their houses and apartments. New terraces and plantings appeared; new electrical and water lines where laid down main streets; and roads were blacktopped, striped in white, and lined with reflectors. Yet old ways linger. Many families still tend their own vineyards and olive groves; many keep chickens, rabbits, pigeons, and hunting dogs in pens behind their houses. Hunting for fowl and hare begins in September and for wild boar in November.

In Lecchi

La Bottega: food & house-wares & phone, run by Palmira Rinaldi. Open all year, every day 7:30–1:00, 3:30–7:00.
Next door, *Paolo's Bar*: wine shop, coffee, bar & lunch, run by Paolo Cioni. Open every day, all day May through October.
Both Bottega and Bar closed Wednesday & Sunday at noon.
tel. 0577 746021

Borgolecchi: delightful bed & breakfast inn, rooms, apartments, run by Anna Lena Caldara.
tel. 0577 746903 fax 0577 746814
website: www.borgolecchi.com
e-mail: caltur@tiscalinet.it

Malborghetto: lunch & dinner, run by Simone Muricci. Closed Tuesday, open every day July through September.
tel. 0577 746201 website: www.malborghetto.com

Ceramic Workshop of Lies Robbertsen: unique & delicate designs painted, fired, and sold there. Fine leather work by Alessandro Stella. Visits and special orders welcome. Open 10:00 to 12:00, 3:30 to 6:00. Closed Sundays.
tel. 0577 738663

Richard Mello: paintings & prints, visits by appointment, spring & fall.
tel. & fax 0577 746084 e-mail: howmell@aol.com

Castle of Monteluco a Lecchi
(mohn.teh.loo.koh ah lehk.kee)

The castle is the private residence above Lecchi, with six owners, so please walk up the hill rather than drive.

At the castle (behind its tall tower), you can see to the east, across the valley, the long walls of the Brolio Castle (under the crest of high hills), then slightly southward the hilltop Cacchiano Castle (almost hidden behind cypress trees), and below that the square tower of Tornano Castle. To the south, below Monteluco's hill, lie the houses of San Sano and (high in a dip in the farthest hills) the towers of Siena.

The castle first appears in records of the late 10th century. A Ricasoli Firidolfi holding, Monteluco became a Florentine fort in 1176. Strategically sited, it overlooked the valley down which soldiers marched in the incessant wars with Siena. In the early 1500s, the castle endured its severest batterings, inflicted by troops of Siena and the Holy Roman Emperor. However, in 1555 Siena capitulated to troops of Florence. No longer a strategic fort, the nearly destroyed Monteluco was abandoned. Then, over the centuries, *contadini* families moved into its remains.

In the 1960s and '70s, families in the castle and tower moved down into the village of Lecchi where post-war apartments provided more comfortable living. The Baron and Baroness Ricasoli renovated the old fort, installing running water, indoor bathrooms, and the required anti-earthquake bands at the top of the buildings. Today, there are six private dwellings. Each owner has a parcel of land on the hill, where the ancient walled terraces have been saved—an increasingly rare sight, as terraces are being torn down to accommodate today's agricultural machinery (see page 69).

Village of San Sano
(sahn <u>sah</u>.no)

Leaving Lecchi village, drive down the road to the right of the yellow community center, *il circolo.* Halfway down the hill, a sign marks the very sharp right turn to San Sano. Entering San Sano, park along the street and walk in.

You will see a little frog statue. On its left are former farm buildings, now converted into the attractive Hotel Residence San Sano; on the right is the lane that takes you past a fine *trattoria (traht.toh.<u>ree</u>. ah)* and beyond to the small Romanesque church. You can walk in a pleasant circle through this tiny hamlet.

La Grotta della Rana: trattoria and food shop, run by Remo & Adelina Pianigiani, lunch & dinner, terrace. Closed Wednesday.
tel. 0577 746020

Hotel Residence San Sano: run by Heidi & Giancarlo Matarazzo, dinner for its guests, pool. Open all year.
tel. 0577 746130 fax 0577 746156 e-mail: hotelsansano@chiantinet.it

Drive out on the road to the left of the frog statue. In about one mile, turn right onto a gravel road toward Vagliagli. When it dead-ends, turn right to Vagliagli. Along the way, beside the road, you will see a row of olive trees that were not killed by the 1985 freeze — not a common sight.

For an interesting diversion, turn right into the driveway of Dievole vineyard. At a white arrow, turn right. From the parking lot, enjoy a wonderful panoramic view. In the landscape, see if you can locate San Sano village (middle), Monteluco Castle (above to left), Cacchiano Castle (higher to right).

Fattoria Dievole: wine tasting on terrace & tours. Best by appointment, but drop-in is possible in high season.
tel. 0577 322613 fax 0577 322574 website: www.dievole.it
Villa Dievole: many rooms, suites.
tel. 0577 322632 fax 0577 321018 e-mail: villadievole@iol.it

Village of Vagliagli
(vah.lyee.ah.lyee)

Coming into the village you will see how modern apartment buildings are often designed in the Chianti. Park at the edge of the old center.

This is a good village in which to mark the changes that were made over the centuries in walls, doorways, and windows. There is a bar where you might have a sandwich made and then relax at a table on its terrace in front. Across the way is a food shop, Alimentari Rovai. On the facade of the church is St Christopher, staff in hand, who looks back onto his shoulder at the Christ Child who is blessing him. On Via di Calcinaia there is St Anthony with the Child. Off Piazza Vittorio Emanuele (King of Italy as of the 1860s), you can walk through a little tunnel on the left.

In Vagliagli

Bar I Manganelli: drinks, sandwiches made to order, ice cream bars.

La Taverna: restaurant on Via del Sergente, lunch & dinner. Closed Monday evening and Tuesday during the winter time.
tel. 0577 322532 fax 0577 321842

Driving on, you will pass Fattoria della Aiola, where wine tasting is also offered.

San Giusto in Salcio Parish Church
(sahn j<u>oos</u>.toh een <u>sahl</u>.choh)

After driving north some four miles, turn right toward Lecchi. Right away, there is a small sign on the right for San Giusto in Salcio. Turn in and park near the church. The church is open weekdays and for Sunday mass at 12:00. Or, look for someone to let you into the church and offer a contribution.

San Giusto's simple facade with arched doorway, its curved apse at the back, and, inside, its central nave with two side aisles typify the Romanesque style. Around the doorway and round window, and on the tower behind, stones are squared and precisely fitted in the medieval manner. Elsewhere, over centuries of patching, stonework is more random. Inside, the simplicity and soft light lend themselves to sitting quietly, shedding bothersome thoughts, and contemplating the impressive crucifix, carved by Matthew Spender, a sculptor living in San Sano.

The large building right of the church once welcomed clerics. A Florentine friend told us that he came here as a boy to visit his uncle, a priest, who with other priests was in a retreat here (hunting party?). He described an unforgettable winter feast of wild boar and pheasant.

Country Walks

On the road from San Giusto to Lecchi in Chianti, there are lovely walks. (For comments on landscape, turn to the following pages.)

On the road to San Polo in Rosso, you can find places to pull off, not blocking farm roads. This picturesque walk leads to the fine restaurant, Il Poggio, on the left. Across the road, there is a cooking school where guests have a great time. The private road continues to San Polo in Rosso Castle. Its wines are sold in a wine shop in Lecchi.

Il Poggio: restaurant run by Giannetto Catinari & family, lunch & dinner, terrace. Closed Monday.
tel. 0577 746135 or 0577 746176

Podere le Rose, Poggio San Polo 2: one-week or one-day cooking classes. Rooms, apartments, Italian classes.
tel. 0577 746152 fax 0577 2396887
website: www.cpv.it/chianti e-mail: info@cpv.it

For Ama, park immediately on the left as you turn in and walk the gravel road either to Montebuoni's cluster of condominiums remodeled from farm buildings or to Castello di Ama—both giving you wonderful views of Chianti woods, vineyards, and olives. Ama's castle was destroyed centuries ago, but lovely buildings remain. Ama's wines are sold at Paolo's Bar in Lecchi.

Along the Way

Farmhouses, Tabernacles, Old Stone Walls

It is worth a trip to the Chianti countryside just to see the slanting sun strike the warm ochre walls of a stone farmhouse and barn in the early morning or late day.

Many of these wonderful, large houses have been converted into vacation homes, but once in a while you come across one in its original state — built in the 1800s or earlier. Farmhouses are often three stories tall, housing animals and farm implements below and families above. Huge farmhouses shelter several families, and outside staircases to upper levels are common. Often there is a little tower on top, a dovecote with open holes, where pigeons can be snatched from inside to be cooked for dinner. Older farmhouses were once fortified and some still have a standing tower.

An open, covered area is often added to the house, roofed in tile. The outdoor oven is located there, along with tables for preparing food and eating in cool shade. A local woman told me that for her family of nine children she baked twenty-six loaves each week, all in one day in the outdoor oven—and she had had enough of it!

Almost always near the farmhouse there is a stone barn, *capanno*. You know it by the way it is ventilated with openings that are crisscrossed in tiles. Usually these barns were built on a slope so that the back side is two or three stories tall. Barns have a low-walled threshing floor in front, paved in flat stones. Grain was beaten on that floor, the straw tossed into the capanna through the arched front door. The grain was stored there, too. Once Richard and I saw dried beans being threshed this way, but of course nowadays harvesting machines process crops—and barns have become guest houses.

There might be animal stalls in a separate barn, *stalla*, with mangers that have ceramic bowls set into them for water. There are low stone shelters, with stone-walled corrals in front for pigs and sheep—pigs for salami, sausage, and *prosciutto*, sheep for fleece, milk, and pecorino cheese. Somewhere on the property—set into the wall of a house, barn, or post—there will be a small shrine.

Tabernacles—shrines on roadsides, farm lanes, driveways or houses—remind us that this has been a Catholic country since Rome's Emperor Constantine declared it Christian in the 300s. On walks, you might like to compare tabernacles. Which are a major manifestation of faith, which a humble gesture? Is there a statue or a plaque? What sort of flowers and candles are there? Are you moved to pick a flower and place it there? Often there are tabernacles plus two churches in a village—a small medieval chapel and a larger, later church. This is true in the villages of Volpaia and Lecchi in Chianti. In Lecchi, 5:00 mass at the end of the day is held in the little medieval church, but Sunday services, baptisms, communions, and funerals are held in the larger 19th-century church.

Every village has its cemetery. You see its walls as you drive by or see its dozens of tiny lights as you pass at night. You can enter cemeteries through gates that are closed loosely with a chain. Walking in, you see that graves have the favorite (or only) photo, the little lights, and flowers pushed into tall vases. Fresh flowers are placed each weekend, bought from vans that travel to rural villages. As long as there are relatives in the region, the departed are never forgotten. Before November 2, All Souls' Day, people buy enormous chrysanthemums. The blossoms are sometimes six inches across. Cemeteries are a mass of color. The chrysanthemum is the funereal flower, but now it creates a celebration.

You might make comparisons of various Chianti walls, a study in themselves. Many old ones are dry walls, stacked expertly, without mortar. Stones of walls held in place with cement are either placed with the mortar kept back from the surface so that the shapes and textures of the stones are lively, or have mortar coming to the front surface so that the wall is smooth. Walls are sometimes protected on top by bricks laid like a peaked roof, sometimes by flat pavers, sometimes concrete.

Old walls bleach to bright white. On these, I like to trace with my hand the weathered patterns of grey, ochre, and black lichen—miniscule landscapes. Growing out of crevices you find small ferns, poppies, runaway oats, and ivy. You will meet shy little lizards sunning themselves on the warm stones, and darting away as you come near. Children try to catch them and never succeed.

Chianti's Landscape

The explorations in this book take you through beautiful southern Chianti. Once, this was the region of the Etruscan civilization and then of the ancient Romans, but little evidence can be seen. We see evidence of the Christian era, of medieval and later days.

While driving along or taking peaceful walks, it is hard to imagine that this region was the setting for almost endless wars. Centuries of conflict explain the fortified architecture of houses, villages, and castles—forms that we cherish today as hallmarks of Tuscany's beauty. Let me spend a moment on warfare because it not only helps us understand the landscape, but also helps us appreciate and celebrate the enormous achievements of the Tuscan people in spite of conflict.

Briefly, there were the waves of so-called barbarians who brought down the Roman Empire by the late 400s. Then during the following centuries there were endless contests between Tuscan fiefdoms and incessant wars during the Middle Ages and Renaissance.

There were a number of major players in the battles that ravaged Chianti from the 1100s into the mid 1500s. Two of them were the city-states of Florence and Siena which fought for control of the Chianti—its rich wine, oil, and grain, its commercial centers, and its trading routes.

The Popes in Rome and the Holy Roman Emperors in Germany were also major combatants. At first the Papacy allied itself with Germanic kings and with Emperors, beginning with Charlemagne in 800. But during successive centuries, papal troops fought these Holy Roman Emperors for land, wealth, power, and control of Italy. Each side allied itself with first one city-state and then another.

City-states periodically called on France for support, but at one point France itself invaded Italy. In the late 1400s, the Spanish, who already ruled the Kingdoms of Sicily and Naples, were led by King Alphonse of Aragon in invading the Chianti region—laying siege to many of the fortified towns and outlying castles you visit.

In 1520, Charles V, King of Spain, became the Holy Roman Emperor. Forces of the Emperor, the Pope, Florence, and Siena—in shifting alliances that included other city-states and hired mercenaries—inflicted on Chianti open battles, long sieges, devastation of farmlands, famine, and worse. In the 1500s, the cannon caused ruination.

Every fortified castle you visit on these itineraries was aligned with Florence and located on the front line in these battles with Siena and its allies. It is a wonder that anything has survived. It is little wonder that in the repeatedly mended farm and village houses the owners barred doors, shuttered their windows, and lived upstairs. Owners of castles built and rebuilt walls and towers. It is astonishing and moving to notice that, for all the patching and reconstruction during these harrowing centuries, a love of beauty endured. You walk through a graceful arch, duck under stones of a carefully shaped doorway, marvel at a gentle fresco, stop to admire an elegant belltower.

Peace in the Chianti came finally when stalwart Siena was conquered by Florence in 1555—with the help of imperial forces that combined Spanish and German troops. The Emperor—with the Pope—chose a member of the Florentine Medici family to rule all of Tuscany, including Siena.

Three centuries of relative peace followed 1555. You see castles that were rebuilt as villas rather than forts. Wealthy Florentines and Sienese commissioned country villas on large acreages. Peace in the region was interrupted only briefly by Napoleon in the early 1800s. Italy became a unified nation in the 1860s, with Florence as its capital and Bettino Ricasoli its second prime minister.

The traditional economic system of Tuscany was sharecropping. The land was owned by the aristocracy but worked by the peasants, *contadini*. The *contadini* families produced diversified products—grain, milk and cheese, meat, wine, and oil—that were divided evenly with the landowners who, in turn, supplied the land, farm buildings, and seeds. This system came to an end after World War II.

The War devastated the Chianti's agricultural economy. Peasants fled to the cities and farms were vacated. As a result, the agricultural economy shifted to single-crop wine production—and some olive oil—with hired workers. Abandoned farmhouses and outbuildings were converted into the vacation retreats, inns, and hotels you see today.

Walking in the Chianti Countryside

Among the world's loveliest places to walk is the Chianti region, and so we have included in each itinerary a place to pull off for a short stroll. But any roadside walk will do.

Hallmarks of the Chianti landscape are the tall, slim cypress trees and the spreading umbrella pines— though neither is native. They came long ago from the eastern Mediterranean. Be that as it may, the sight of either one, bordering a long driveway or outlining the crest of a hill can take your breath away. And there are other magnificent trees.

The Chianti's oak forests cover whole hill-sides, whole valleys. In the warm seasons, forests are dark green—in contrast to the beautiful patterns of fields cleared for light green grape vines and silvery olive trees. As fall creeps toward winter, the forests slowly turn yellow, orange, and mocha—in contrast to the golden vineyards and shimmering olives.

If you stand a while in one spot, you can watch the shadows of clouds pass over this landscape, highlighting, then darkening patches of forests and fields. In early morning, you can watch the fog burn off from the valleys; a house suddenly appears, a barn, a bridge.

The most common oak has a delightful, tiny leaf. In any season, I cut armfuls of oak branches to stuff into a bucket in the stairwell, or I spread boughs on a window sill, with fruit and nuts tucked in. As a symbol of strength and endurance, the oak offers reassurance—especially on a bad day. You cannot miss the sight of oak trees covered with lichen. Once, lichen was harvested for packing material. Today it runs free, yet the oaks survive.

Once in a while you see the revered, evergreen holm oak, large with shiny, dark-green leaves. I thought it was holly until someone showed me its slim, dark acorns. Every so often you come across a stand of aspen trees. One legend has it that the holm oak was the tree of Christ's cross. Another is that the leaves of the aspen tree tremble because it was the tree on which Christ died.

If you spot a mulberry tree, you will like its varied, fanciful leaves.

As you drive along, you will see groves of walnut trees, some very new, laid out in strict rows, destined for lumber. Walnut is prized. In antique and furniture stores, anything of walnut, *noce*, is costly.

In late October into November, prickly brown balls drop onto the road. They fall from the tall chestnut trees with their large, serrated leaves. Don't pick up the balls without gloves. Rub the hull off with your shoe and look for the two or three shiny chestnuts inside. Make a cut through each hull—to prevent explosions—and roast them.

Among leaves, the most intriguing are the fig leaves. Think of Adam. And Eve. The great, green leaves unfold into endless variations of the basic curvaceous shape. It is a terrible loss when they begin to cartwheel away in late fall winds.

In the forests, local owners cut firewood. Even now many houses have no central heat or are just putting it in as gas lines come into the villages. Often people cook at both a gas stove and a fireplace—we do. The fireplace is just right for sausages, a roasted hen, chestnuts.

Everywhere that is uncultivated, thorny bushes grow, called *macchie*. They form a nasty, impenetrable underbrush that the thick-skinned and rough-bristled wild boars love. Families of boar are safe there, and come out mostly at night. Around our olive trees, boars dig for fennel roots. They nibble all the ripe, lower bunches from the grape vines. To control the number of boars (and eat well), squads of 15 men hunt wild boar from November into winter. They bring in many hefty beasts in a season. Except on Tuesdays and Fridays when boars cannot be hunted, wear bright colors on walks in forests; a neighbor's cat came home on three legs.

Along roadsides, you will come across rosemary with its lavender flowers and lavender with its purple flowers, both growing as large bushes. There are hedges of laurel, wild roses, and blackberries. Over whole hillsides you will see the long stems of broom, *ginestra*, with their yellow blossoms. All these colorful plants scent the air, especially after a rain.

In springtime, the early white and yellow crocus blossoms appear. A field can be sprinkled with the tiny *margherita* whose daisy-like blossom is white with a yellow center. Then, and at all seasons, a short, pungent mint, *nepitella*, with small lavender blossoms scents the air, especially after mowing. The purple *malva*, with its geranium-like blossom and leaf, is everywhere, picked by some for a tea that settles the stomach and relieves rheumatism.

Beginning in May, the several varieties of red and orange poppies blossom on their slim, bobbing stems. They pop up between rocks, along the top of walls, across entire fields. The blossom is transparent; where one petal overlaps another they double the color. You want them never to fade. Petals are so delicate that even soft, spring breezes blow them off, leaving the black, spidery centers to stand alone. At this time, the Queen Anne's lace is out and a tall-stemmed flower with a blossom like a dandelion—a festive combination of reds, whites, and yellows.

Through the summer, June into September, the deep purple, pea-family vetch climbs into everything it can—and likewise the wild, white morning glory. This is the season for flowers in the purple, white, and yellow hues. Some blossoms are so tiny you have to squat down to appreciate them. On the other hand, fields of waist-high sunflowers are almost blinding when the huge blossoms turn toward you and the sun at the same time.

In October, a neighbor left on our porch a long spray, binding together deep-green ivy, golden oak leaves with mahogany acorns, silvery branches dangling maroon olives, and long-stemmed rosemary and lavender—a glorious gift.

During the fall, you see the rich yellows of the wildflower we know as butter and eggs, the lovely blue chicory, the bright yellow goldenrod. The berries of firethorn ripen to deep red and so do the round puffy fruit of the strawberry tree, *corbezzolo*. By now, sunflowers hang their heads and turn almost black. Just as the crop looks hopeless, it is harvested for oil.

Wintertime offers the long view. All but the oak and evergreens drop all their leaves, so from the road you can now see farms, castles, and fields that were hidden before. Olive trees drop only a few of their leaves, so their rows of rounded forms still pattern the hillsides, along with the vineyards' black stems and chestnut poles.

yellow ochre

raw sienna

raw umber

burnt umber

burnt sienna

Plowed fields await new vines, olive trees or grains. The overturned clods, on one field after another, present a palette of earthy tones used in paints. The pigments bear local names: raw sienna (as from Siena but spelled with double 'n') and burnt sienna (actually burned), raw umber (as from Umbria) and burnt umber, and the yellow ochres. From these fields we have collected earth and made rather muddy watercolors—a nice messy thing to do with children.

Chianti's Vineyards

The appearance of Chianti's vineyards has changed radically in the last few years. Until recently, the hilly slopes of the Chianti were terraced. Along the length of terraces, olive trees were planted, and often grape vines were strung between them. The flat surface of terraces held the soil and conserved the water that enabled grain to grow there, too. Grain, grapes, and olives were harvested there—the bread, wine, and oil that have sustained Tuscan life for centuries.

Until as recently as fifty years ago or so, oxen could both graze and pull plows along these terraces. Oxen gave way to small tractors; strung-out grape vines gave way to enormous vineyards; and grain harvests gave way to commercial growers and bakeries. Now the terraces themselves have given way to modern agricultural methods.

You might hear the bulldozers that are bringing down terrace walls—old walls that are already tumbling and would cost a fortune to rebuild. Certainly you will see piles of the leftover rocks. The narrow, varied, and stony terraces made sense in the days of oxen. Today mechanized tractors, wagons, sprayers, and pickers require a specific width between rows of vines.

Well-organized rows are planted running downhill. If you were raised on contour farming, as I was, this can drive you crazy. But it provides more stable driving of vehicles than if the rows ran crosswise. In the long run, whether the erosion that pulls soil away at the top and piles it at the bottom will create problems remains to be seen. Maybe not. Vines put down deep roots.

You might also see or hear the immense machines that are breaking up and pulling out ledges of rock from the fields. Roots of new vines are going into very welcoming soil. The gargantuan rocks are piled by earth-moving equipment into trim walls that cut across and stabilize downhill vineyards. They seem to have been built by giants—and are handsome. In fact, though it is heartwarming to see a hillside where terraces are painstakingly preserved, the new landscape is beautiful, too. And it is good to know that new agricultural methods help to bring a higher standard of living than ever before to Tuscan farmers.

The winter grape vines are pruned back to their stems or trunks. They scrawl a dark calligraphy, almost spooky, against the bare earth. In early spring, tiny fuzzy buds poke out. Slowly, pale and vulnerable green leaves unfold, followed by scrawny bunches of bee-size grapes.

Through summer months, bunches of grapes grow fat. Some are cut away to strengthen the quality of those that remain. Leaves that block sun and air from the grapes are pulled off. Mold is the enemy, next to hail.

In early fall, the white grapes are picked and dried for the Tuscan sherry, *Vinsanto*. The basic grapes for Chianti Classico wine, Sangiovese, have become deep purple. From late September into early October, harvesting is done when weather is dry. Moisture can seep into grapes and dilute the alcohol content.

All of us, at harvest time, go row by row with clippers in hand, cutting off the bunches of grapes and tossing them into crates. Crates are spilled into machines that pull off the grapes, spit out the stems, and send the grape mash along tubes into tanks to ferment. Eventually the wine goes into casks to age.

Very large vineyards sometimes resort to picking with machines. The machines shoot grapes out into a truck that follows, and shoot stems out in another direction. You hear the machines from miles away, gobbling across the land.

You will see that some vineyards are protected with fences or low electrified wires, but wild boars find the unprotected grapes. In November and December, village men take sweet revenge when they hunt wild boar, *cinghiale (cheen.gee.ah.leh)*. Cooks make a rich hunters' stew, a real *cacciatora*, and wash the wild boar down with Chianti wine. Probably you won't be hunting, skinning, quartering, and simmering your own 250-pound boar, so be sure to order cinghiale in a restaurant.

In late October, vineyards begin to turn lovely colors—deeper greens, shimmering golds, copper, and warm rusts. Vines of certain sorts turn bright red. In November, leaves turn into tissue paper, rustle in the wind, and are blown away.

Chianti's Olive Groves

The appearance of olive groves is not at all what it was some fifteen years ago and for decades earlier.

When you see a large, single olive tree, it is a rare survivor of the freeze, thaw, and re-freeze of January, 1985. Inhabitants say they could hear the trees groaning. This disaster killed almost all of Tuscany's olive trees. Among the four kinds of trees that are typically planted together, only the *leccino* olive survived, plus a few others in sheltered spots.

Across the entire region, the dead trees were cut down at the base. You can see their stumps. When new shoots sprang from the old roots, the strongest two or three shoots were left to grow into the groupings you see now. Sometimes new, single trees were planted. After some five or six years, they began to produce. Now, both the trees you see with two or three main trunks and the new single trees have diameters of about six to eight inches. They have filled out into the checkered pattern you see on the Chianti's hillsides.

Each year, the market for Tuscan oil prompts landowners to clear land and plant new little trees—skinny things supported by poles, laid out geometrically on land cleared of terraces. The spaces between rows are geared to mechanized equipment. In new olive groves, irrigation tubes run alongside the plants.

It can stop your heart to see how drastically olive trees are pruned, usually in late winter. The center of each tree is hollowed out so that sun and breezes can move through the branches. In early autumn, there is a light pruning. When the fruitless growth and suckers are cut away, trees look like forlorn sheared sheep—but recover in a few weeks.

Richard and I begin to harvest our olives when other villagers do, in middle to late November. This is earlier than in southern Italy where olives are left to mature until they drop. Here, the belief is that olives picked before full maturity produce a light, fruity oil.

Villagers taught us how to harvest the olive trees that came with the house we bought. Fifteen years ago, we picked in the traditional way with World War II parachutes spread under the trees. On a windy day, the parachutes flipped about and the olives sailed into the grass. Recently, we and most everyone else have replaced parachutes with nets that stay put.

As our hands strip down each branch, olives pop off onto the nets. Not many leaves follow. If a tree has only a few olives, we skip laying out a net and pop the olives into a basket hung from our shoulder or strapped across our belly. After each day of picking, we spread the green, maroon, and black olives—only three inches deep—on the floor of a dry, brick cellar. Mold is ruinous.

The reservation at the olive mill has been set long before—for instance, at the *frantoio* in Volpaia or another near Vertine. We bag or crate our olives and transport them to the mill's grinding wheels, oil extractors, and machines that spin off water. At the end of the process, a glorious, chartreuse stream of pungent oil falls into stainless steel cans. We store cans of oil in our cool cellar, *cantina*.

There is nothing like the flavor of the new oil. Immediately, we toast slices of Tuscan bread, rub them with garlic cloves, and drench them in the oil. This is *bruschetta* (*broos.keht.tah*), also called *fettunta* (*feht.toon.tah*), sometimes dressed up with chopped tomato, onion, and fresh basil.

We hope you will have this ancient and incomparable treat often—with new oil or not. *Buon appetito! Auguri!*

Paintings by Richard Mello

Heartfelt thanks for help go to Egle Cioni, Charles Ewell, Barbara Giuffrida, Nancy Leszczynski, Malcolm Lucard, Belinda and Robin Mello, Ann McFarlane. Thanks go, too, to the incomparable staff of the publisher Mandragora in Florence.

R. Mello 2000

Printed by Alpilito – Firenze
February 2003